MELODIOUS WOMEN

MELODIOUS WOMEN

BY

MARJORIE AGOSIN

TRANSLATED FROM THE SPANISH BY

MONICA BRUNO GALMOZZI

Latin American Literary Review Press
Pittsburgh, Pennsylvania
Series: Discoveries
1997

The Latin American Literary Review Press publishes Latin American creative writing under the series title Discoveries, and critical works under the series title Explorations.

Library of Congress Cataloging-in-Publication Data

Agosín, Marjorie.
    [Mujeres melodiosas.   English]
    Melodious women / by Marjorie Agosín ; translated by Monica
    Bruno.
            p.   cm. -- (Discoveries)
    ISBN 0-935480-91-9 (pbk.)
    I. Bruno, Monica.   II. Title.   III. Series.
    PQ8090. 1.G6M8413   1997
    861--dc21   97-42693
                                                    CIP

Cover art by Roser Bru.

Published by:
Latin American Literary Review Press
121 Edgewood Avenue
Pittsburgh, PA 15218

*For Sonia,
Josephine,
and
Frida*

*To women,
To life…*

CONTENTS

SISTERS

THE CITIES OF WOMEN

HAPPINESS

TITANIA'S CREED

I

I would rule
with a council
of violet fairies,
with the smell of lilacs and patchouli,
dancers in the
fragility,
of the peace
of tulle.

II

I would guide myself
by scent, like a
presence.

III

I could converse with
the dead,
I would hear the true tone,
I would ask them, the fairies,
for the gifts necessary
for proper government:
a little piece of unconditional
happiness
other branches of sanity.

IV

I would follow their advice
like the necessity
of learning to name
the stars,
the extinct trees,
all that which is ambiguous and gentle

and the walking through the thickness
of the mauve nights.

V

I would rule
from a hot air balloon,
I would not have palaces nor dark offices,
only the sky.
They say that there is much peace and silence
in the heights.
I would install my council of fairies
behind a willow,
behind a crystal.
I would serve water from the green rivers
like the warmest wine to the warm throats.

VI

I would surround myself with the fairies, with all presence
that are breath,
golden seeds
in the darkness.

VII

There would be no borders,
only the eyes
of the just.

VIII

I would wear white,
I would hand out almonds
and pigeons,
chocolates
without borders,
in a dream of thresholds.

ALICIA:
to Alicia Alonso

Alicia,
it is not true
that you do not see.
That you move
groping in the dark
in the scenarios
streaked in darkness.
Alicia you do see
beyond the nests,
beyond the light,
and your feet
are not legs,
they are the swallows
fleeting as if in a frenzy
in love with the earth
of the islands.
My Alicia
with fish's feet
and the water's gaze,
you are the most illuminated
of all Cassandras
when you dance
you resurrect all the dead of the Caribbean
and your illuminated Havana.
When you laugh,
your eyes burst,
they are two repositories,
caves
of all the chrysalis
of all the
islands
re-encountered.

ANTIGONE

I

Ancient
pious Antigone
ancient damsel
among the shadows
elemental, pious
among the abysses.

II

Beloved,
elliptical,
you disobeyed for pity,
for the most absolute
conscience which is the faith
and the word.
You buried your dead,
you gave them a residence of earth.

III

Among the moans of the dead
you mingled with the delirium of the living
the most beautiful prayers to God and the devil.
More than your time and your life Antigone,
you offered consciences
the honor of the Kiddush
of the veil,
of the handful of soil.

IV

You did not want the outdoors,
the horror of combat,
to leave them without words
and among the abandon of love
you sang to that dead
who is the dead
of all women
which is the angel of all the skies.

V

Condemned lineage
anxious damsel,
tree among the ashes,
you are the offering, the flower on the lighthouse vessels
the name and the most sublime poem
and alone you disembarked the wrath of men
the specter of the Gods.

VI

Singer,
friend of the travelers,
creatress of paths,
we called you during the nights
of horror's insomnia
we called you during the
indifferent time of the
shrouds,
you arrive winged like faith
with the most sublime secret of words.

VII

You are deep like the deepest sorrow
or the flames of the desert in the heart of the
uninhabited.
Antigone, my life,
you did not want the dead to feel cold,
to descend with the verses of love to
the most perfidious darkness.

VIII

It was your life that gave life,
there in the most staggering thickness of the
darkness where the Gods
do not mask their wrath
where men-birds
are enveloped in an infamous fugue.

IX

Rigorous in your truth
spellbound in the faith of breath
like an illuminated wind:
the silence
of the dead.

ARIADNE

I

I unwove my weaving
and like all those crazy women
who await
in the moist fire
of certain love letters.
I unwove and planned
your shroud
knowing you were alive
and that you played with the enchantments
of oblivion

II

I was like all of them
those who wait
in the sites
of death
those who wait in the hallways
uninhabited by hunger.
I was like all of them
and like none at the same time.

JOSEPHINE BAKER

I

Josephine
with your velvet tongue,
arms like one
naked body,
your nakedness,
like the chrysalis,
like the butterflies that
do not blink before the surprise.

II

From your body that
is like a sugarcoated coast,
that shivers and never watches.

III

Josephine what beauty you are before the
open skin of love,
what valor in exile,
to leave America
and to be black again.

UMILIANA CÁRDENAS:
FISHER OF POETS

From
the time
of the sirens
and the ceremonial fishermen,
all wet and full of song
with her years filled
with scales
of unbelievable
fragrances and the
transient stones,
she emerges from the sea
Umiliana Cárdenas
precarious and oversized.
She offers us poems
for fifty pesos each
and fifty recipes
to cook potatoes.
She is from the islands that are more islands than the sky,
where the wind foresees
births and deaths,
where life is a golden corner
of orange blossoms and unspoken times.

LEONORA CARRINGTON

Owner of the dominions,
of the Celt's time,
of Ireland, green and golden
Leonora traveler,
astronomer in love
with celestial hyenas.
You are and are not the portrait
of the nomadic memory.
Your body is a vault
moistened among the memories,
a code of brilliant canvases.

II

Leonora
what are you looking for behind the magic
of the brush?
Leonora, where do you cut the imaginary scraps?
where do you live, Leonora?
in what threshold can you return to your dreams?
Leonora beloved traveler,
friend of the condors and the pigeons,
how do you travel in the darkened shadows?
you are like the floating islands that play
in the distance.

III

Beloved Leonora,
I close my eyes and I do not stop
seeing you.
You are there with your violet drinks,
with your alchemies and resplendent fissures,
with your hair like the fastest horse

Leonora you are all the clearings in the forests
the elves of Ireland
the secret moss of Chiapas
the magical
wind,
traveler
with full wine glasses
and light blue ribbons
in your hair.

RACHEL CARSON

I

In the forest's clearing,
in the agile roundness of light
you are fluorescent
like the most daring and calm leaf
like the dreams of the fireflies.
Guardian of time,
namer of water and dry rivers,
of the rivers of thunder,
in your hands you carry
the immense gestures
the beating of the wind
the pure gaze of perseverance.

II

Friend of birds,
of the silence of all forests,
you are a chunk of living water,
the most perpetual cadence in those immense streets,
guardian of secrets,
respectful like the infinite which is sublime.

III

You are a woman
full, joyful
surprised and simple
your hand is like a ring
sliding over the barks
of the earth.

IV

You suspected the merchants
to be false emperors,
you predicted their infamies,
the trees of Brazil,
the errant birds of Bengal,
and you only asked
for a time to inhabit yourself,
a cease-fire for our planet.

ROSARIO CASTELLANOS

I

Traveler
of the tired hours and
the ashen temple,
is it true that you remained
suspended in nothingness
"like a cloud, like the perturbed
and delirious rock?"

II

Among the thresholds,
silent, amber of dreams,
yes, there was another way Rosario, beloved,
loving Rosario,
something beyond Valium
the monthly hemorrhage,
the days of insomnia and empty moons.

Your verses
were leafy
trees,
uncertain roads
where the healers nested
in the century plant.

How premature, premeditated your death
in the foreign lands,
in the ship of the exiled,
in a pilgrimage of the dead.
Alone in Jerusalem, Rosario, there
like a stolen Christ.

Alone, Rosario without a rosary
alone in all the abysses.

Rosario there was another way to be,
to live, to die.

CLEAR CLARICE:
To Clarice Lispéctor

I

Clarice
beloved,
making, with words,
deserts, paths,
a clear saying
on the breaths.

II

Braiding the
words into schemes,
breaths of life.
With your hands,
extended like a
word that travels and burns
like a word
inhabited by birds
and oaks
that is how you are Clarice, all stretched out and beautiful.

III

How can we approach truth,
the times of the skin,
words like rejoicing and piety,
the words
of joy and of the
silences?

DELMIRA:
To Delmira Agustini

I

Haunted and feverish
delirious, hurt Delmira
with the verses and the swords of Eros.
The foolish men have come to see you
only in death,
and with the distance
of a lack of love,
you are an extended and pious rock.
They photograph you naked, gagged,
violating the last site of peace.
They do not cover you,
they want you to be mean and naked,
but now you are even more beautiful.

II

Your verse is filled with roses and poppies
when pronouncing you,
Delmira you sleep,
the living follow you,
they carry out loud
your biography
they inhabit the coffers of your voice
they are envious to the point of idleness,
Delmira of our dreams,
they claim to have loved you,
read you, at half-light,
but you, clever and wise Delmira,
know that you only
belonged
to words,

to the texture of their lineage
to the most strident fragrance
of the verb that
is the key, river, golden water.

ISADORA DUNCAN

I

Isadora cloudy and luminous,
in the savage fog,
and ungainly,
how long was your hair
like a beheaded stork?
in which legend
did they tell you
to undo your hair?

II

In this spring
of insomniac sleeping pills,
you approach love
on tiptoe,
your body in a circle where the velocity
of that which is earthly nests.

III

Your arms, beloved Isadora
are two domes where no time
finds its defeat.
like the most fleeting
of fogs,
like the most opportune guest,
you turn your feet
into mouthfuls of smoke, reachable stars.
Your happiness is contagious.
Isadora even the
beggars,
the abandoned ladies,

the fish,
the women by vocation and of idleness,
they clap with their skirts of water,
when they see you, Isadora, all winged
with your foreboding bones.

IV

Among the foliage beyond the light,
my beloved,
dressed with your suit of algae
where did you leave your crown of fire?

ELENA:

to Elena Gascón-Vera

I

In you burn
the birds
the foretold futures
of all Hispanic lands
where the Spanish language
blooms.
You are an indomitable
and tender
barren plains
you are sought by victorious women
who nest
in your honey-filled mouth
and I love you traveling Elena
because you are the most
beautiful and opaque Dulcinea,
erroneous,
the most imperfect
surprised before all windmills
the most beautiful
fig tree.

EMILY DICKENSON
for Diana

At dusk,
when the lights of Amherst
light up shyly,
you arrived to the sinful
social gatherings.

I

You are invisible, like the lamps of love,
with your dresses adorned in moss, white lilies to
lie down together with the night.
You sit behind Lavinia
and you smile.

II

Like the most gentle guest
you move about,
in the solemn roundness of the night.
The stars illuminate your return to the room
of findings,
in the house of your elves,
next to the closet of magic.
You write a letter in which you speak to the world,
you thank them for all the invitations
to events which you judiciously
never assist:
"You will forgive me for I never visit
I am from the fields you know."

III

Emily of the fields of the most alert poppies
cultivator of gardens,
herbalist magician
of orange cilantro,
creatress of sweet imaginings
you are the most indulgent being
before joy
before the space, yours and only yours
where naked you took off your shoes
and you wrote
disheveled and furiously happy.

IV

On Maine Street,
nothing was ever lost
from your happy gaze.
All and none knew you,
although Lavinia desperately wanted to be like you,
with your reddish hair filled with whispers.
Wise and never secluded Emily
it is easier to wear a white dress when speaking with the dead,
it is easier to let them speak in their lost murmurs
because that is how they tell us:
"Do not mind me
if I do not
come with feet, in my
heart I come — talk
the most and laugh
the longest —
when all the rest have gone."

V

I like to dream about you
lying in
the wild
gardens
on the fields like love lamps,
with that which you most love
your words
predestined,
alert and judicious words,
the divine words
resplendent,
sheltering themselves from the incomprehensible murmurs,
the words swinging
in the warm hand
because in them you found
the friends, the
true interlocutors
they did not let you down
they are better company than the vain and
darkened homes of Amherst
the beloved words, Emily,
cover your body like silk
like the
stars in
a tranquil
mirror.

EVE

I

More than to Adam
you belonged to the clay,
to memorable materials,
captive among the grazing fields.
She was shaped in the shadows
of the most alien paradise,
predetermined destinies
and covered her voice with muteness
and prophecies.

II

She walked barefoot and transfigured.
She named the stars,
developed transparencies,
she grew and from them
others grew.
Her split belly engendered
unusual life,
music in the background,
the transparent breath of air.

III

No matter how much the sultans
wished to
undress her,
they found
that her clothes
guarded the attire of all victories
and the more naked she was,
the least untiring,

more extraordinarily sublime she was.
They could not tame her
with their voices.

IV

They beat her,
they abused her,
they gagged her
and they expelled her from the clubs,
the stores,
the classrooms.
They ignored her in history
and they called her bad luck.

IV

Forgetful
without rancor,
she dressed herself,
she walked as if ephemeral,
she inhabited herself
and together with her daughters
She applied to herself and
to them fresh rain.
She wrote her name and that of the others
among the forgetful rocks
and she wrote her life in the bowing waves
of the rivers
of life.
Suddenly
she became
the most fragrant of all
the counties
and the most victorious
star of the night
in the days of blood
and sun.

GALA

I

Evil and oval.
Flying, Gala,
firefly's
voice
and wings of
a fleeting sparrow.
Who are you, Gala?
acute and award-recipient
angel?
Who do you confuse
among the faces,
unequal and beautiful,
horrified and lucid?

II

You are like the dream of that which is not behind the shadows,
you live beyond the sky,
in the meditating roses,
in the air, suspended in light.

III

You are like a simple savage
in your indigo palace,
leaning back to be painted
but you are the
creatress of the canvas,
the hunter of birds,
the dreamer of fish,
she who holds the roses.

FRIDA KAHLO

I

In the startled light,
beyond the footsteps of the living
and the sprinkling of the
dead,
in blue Coyoacán
I arrive to you Frida,
I approach your heart
of your liquid
face
I bless your leopard eyebrows.

II

There you are
tired in the tranquillity of the purple morphine.
The strange visitors
siege your easel,
your back like a limb on fire.

III

There you are
reposed and restless
yearning for the loneliness of silence
of the century plant, the copal,
listening to the gagged rains
in Coyoacán
near the hemlock of love.

IV

Frida
they do not leave you alone
not even in the subtle peace
of death,
they all want
to tear a piece
of your cloth,
of your wounds,
the blue walls
of your home
of your made up figure.
They all want
a postcard with your body
because it is alien to them,
because it is so familiar to them and at the same time
unknown,
curious in its true pain.

V

Today I arrived
to you Frida
of Coyoacán.
I knocked on the cobalt
blue thresholds
in your home where
you received everyone
and no one.
You are asleep in the dreams of ill omens
with the belly filled with fireflies.
Beyond the silence I heard your footsteps,
I heard your moans,
your screams
that said
long life to life.

LEONOR OF AQUITAINE

I

Duchess of Aquitaine
in your skirts, they invented
the languages of desire,
and verse was applied to the lips,
it parted as if by chance
as if by a divine clarity.

II

Translator of omens,
of the chloroform dreams
and the women in love
you lived in all the gestures of the kiss
and its fragrances.

III

With the restraint of the
illuminated
you condemned the
false prophets of love,
you covered the unlucky ones.

IV

Your body Leonor,
queen of France,
was a depository net
of stars.

V

Descendant of Guillaume,
you enter and depart torn and fresh
among the dreams of women
you are the most beloved among the packs of hounds
you are the most invoked in the courts of love and its sorrows.

LILLITH

I

The panthers
smelled your warm and young sex,
the owls illuminated your paths,
the well-known snakes wished to enter the shortness of your breath,

II

Nothing stopped you.
Far from paradise,
there were other paradises.
Your name called itself.
You were pink like the clearing of all caves.
You woke up free outdoors,
the soil on your face,
on your body, filled with happy birds.
Although distant from paradise
you surrounded yourself with pigeons,
you fell asleep illuminated,
you disobeyed,
you were owner of the nights of love
and the days of light.

FLORENCE NIGHTINGALE

Among all the wounds,
the deep howls
of the sick,
the Crimea on fire at the borders
there you were,
winged and erect,
with you steps in the rain, beyond the forbidden shrouds,
intrepid, never abnegate
disobedient
like a gust
among the envies,
like a songbird
among the perturbed abysses of men.

CAMILA O'GORMAN

I

Camila O'Gorman
playing blind chicken
among the shadows,
reading love letters
aloud,
creating the luminosity
of the butterflies.

II

The children, the legends
accompany you
while your name and
your face, Camila O'Gorman
after your death
is never wavering.

III

In the moonlit days,
in the parties of maddened love,
you were lucky
of having a grandmother who still believed in love letters,
saved them like the most brilliant tiara
of the perfidious history
that condemned you
to passing death,
to the tearing of the abyss
before the mediocre
provincial
dictators.

IV

How beautiful you were when you loved
and called Ladislao Gutierrez
as if your voice
were a calendar in no hurry
as if time and its humbleness
belonged to you.

V

You were happy
in the insane and disrespectful love,
happy, away from the spells and the sorcerers,
happy Camila O'Gorman because your naked body was a savage
moistened river.

VI

Today I want to write this love poem to you,
tell you that you are more alive than ever.
The school children
know you,
they pray for you and by you,
they call you by your name
sweet, noble, wild.

VII

Woman in love,
enemy of the roses,
the false thorns,
dignified woman of her era
like a star
among the walls.

PANDORA

I

Because she opened that box
of astonishment and alien to her voice,
they accused her of
the curses, the ills,
all the plagues and the
insomnia
of the sinister
solitudes.

II

She was not inclined
to fear,
nor the sinister capacity
of obedience.
She was what she was:
indomitable,
distant,
transparent.
She dressed in the green hues
of the Gods,
she opened the forbidden box,
brought us
astonishment,
the joy of its truth
the joy of love
hope in the secret paths,
the ambiguity
of breath.

VIOLETA PARRA

I

Violeta of the
Andes, Violeta of the highlands,
Violeta of the Pacific,
indomitable and serene,
you sing
transfigured, you tell us what you call them,
loving the renegades,
the soulless insanity.
"What feelings can,
knowledge cannot."

II

You are a guitar of breaths
and murmurs
a guitar that howls in the darkness
of the absent.
Violeta chilensis.

III

You undress in the heaven of your voice
you are a field of wild blackberries,
a constellation of violets between the sky and the earth.

IV

We remember you now, after death
because you died
of love,
to dance with death
that feared only you.

V

Violeta, you sing
beyond the night and its horizons
as if there were only you
and Violeta,
uninhabited women,
like a guitar, like a hand rocking the
most precious child of absence.

VI

Violeta when you sing,
more than light, I am filled with souls and smokes,
more than your voice
it is your birdlike hands and your lively lutes
your voice like a hurricane
rocking us,
waking us up in the wild
barren plains of our loneliness

PENELOPE

Penelope
with your walk
of rocks and roughness,
your eyes like islands.
With your care like a prayer
who are you calling
in the night of foams and omens?
What courtyard are you going to in your airy heels?
Penelope, who are you
writing
letters to while you
wait?

CHRISTINE DE PISSAN

I

It is you Christine de Pissan
in your city,
in our city,
festive mayor,
an illuminated swallow
in the places
of fire.

II

In your ample skirts
in your gaze beyond the borders
you greet us all
nobles and plebeians
Minerva and Semiramis
Agrippina and Sister Juana
all lit up with your marvelous music boxes
that once opened and entering the city of women
they shine with the sound of women.

III

More than your audacity
more than your spirit like a starched lighthouse
you are sensible Christine,
moderate in your sayings
eloquent never docile
before the servile lords
that invent us
invent you in the portrait of false idleness.

IV

We all arrived
to your city
nobody was lost in your footsteps
nobody aged while waiting for
the food or the
blessings
because they were reunited like tresses, like
rings, we were one woven mantle
and we named ourselves the slaves of the labyrinths,
those forced to give birth, the thirsty midwives,
and we arrived to the splendid city
where the lizards, like children made reverences and signals
and life, Christine, in your city
allowed us to see the oaks
the butterflies
the metaphors of knowledge.
Finally,
in your city we had places
and nobody threw us out
of its contours.
Nobody threw stones at us in
the dense and grave night
finally we were one city of women.

QUEEN ISABEL

I

More than the trips,
her stunts as an eternal ruler,
more than her jewels
and her false depths,
I would like to know
about Columbus and Isabel
the intermittent nights
of austere love,
of warm red love,
of deliriousness and the fragrance,
of spilled wine on the able and fleeting body of love.

II

More than the imaginary arrivals
I want to know about the murmurs
of the room,
of the semi-dark areas
while Columbus and Isabel
peeked at love,
at the New World that they barely
brushed with lips and skin.

QUINTRALA

I

The women say,
so many women,
they say as if in a broken whisper,
they say as if afraid and joyful
that near Melipilla,
at the crack of dawn,
when night enters the clarity of day,
with their chests lit up
like dragons in love
in gallops "Ms. Quintrala,"
queen of insomnia,
owner of all the lands
of the country,
the other Chilean that
with a ring left men mute.
That is what the women of Melipilla say.

II

Mrs. Catalina of the rivers, they called her
when in her carriage she raised the haze,
the fog, the sleepy flowers,
and the women also feared her and made the signs of faith when
they saw her
go by
and the women also
wanted to be she,
to play naked
whip the trees,
love the slaves
look at themselves naked in the streams,
soften the crevices of the body with oil
and violet lotions.

III

They, the women of the town,
they said that in the midst of silence,
that in the midst of the evening prayer
Mrs. Catalina of the rivers arrived
offering herself incense and the faith of sex.
All of this they said,
the women of Melipilla
when the gentlemen arrive in
the modern and antique carriages
to ask where Mrs. Catalina
of the rivers lives.

LAURA RIESCO

I

Astonished,
beyond silence
during this winter
during all winters
Laura, with her bleeding heart
so reddish, so well-loved,
gave me the breath of summer.

II

Lit up and dressed with rivers
she brought me
a basket of flowers,
filled with country things
the white lilies were warm,
the violets were deep and open,
like thankful lamps.
The whole summer was a circle
of poppies in my hands.
Laura brought the lilac and the blue of falling stars.

III

In these country presents,
the hollyhock,
I saw her face,
her hands made of rivers,
and soggy bottoms.
All of her was in bloom
making
the party more splendid in my pupils,
the basket more victorious and loud.

IV

My friend Laura
from Maine
in this winter
of small spells
Laura Riesco
brought me
handfuls of summer
and in her voice
I heard the voice of
my dead friends
in the vigil of lilacs,
in the incarnation of yellow,
I heard the inviting music
of all fields.

V

Their flowers, blooming
looked like
the sea
delirious, spongy,
like the breath of the river dolphins.
In this season to sail through the shadows,
I received
the whole summer
in a wild bunch
of flowers and they were Laura's hands.

LAURA RIESCO II

I

Laura Riesco
carries wreaths
of dead
bouganvilleas
surprised,
she roams,
she falls in love
with the inclines
of the roads like forests
she sings of cinnamon.

II

Laura Riesco
frees herself of that
uncomfortable mask
nobody confuses her with
a prudent woman
one who does not need
nostalgia,
one who does not miss things
she sings forgotten Peruvian waltzes.

III

Laura Riesco,
somewhat aged
and all in mauve
travels through Lima
she stops in the trash
like little fireflies flying around her head
that of an old adolescent
she sings of cinnamon.

IV

Laura Riesco
travels through Lima invaded by rain
the same Lima that Vallejo saw
that of the defeated,
of the *senderistas*[1],
and she does not understand
why she did not return to her fleeting homeland
with winding roads
with elegant beggars
handing out
the knives of love.

V

Laura Riesco
only thinks about Lima
in the rounds,
filled with eagles, with
perturbed noises.

VI

Laura Riesco
thinks about poems
she left
that blue noon, half dark,
under the great buffet,
under the fuchsia drying paper
under the piano's back,
under the bed of
her old aunt
who offered her peace and silver candelabra.

---

[1] *Followers of the terrorist group Sendero luminoso (The Shining Path).*

VIII

Laura Riesco
travels through the streets of Lima,
Amparo's kitchen,
the turbid flower market.
She returns because she never has left
and in the wet streets she
can still hear his footsteps
crossing her shadow.

RIGOBERTA MENCHU

I

Like a flowering
hand
you are
Guatemala
to the South of
light
to the South of air,
stretched out like magical mirrors.

II

You are a land of savage green
colors,
like the moss of love,
you are a hallucinated geography
of human life.

III

I declare my love to you
Guatemala,
I bless all the bells that announce
your deaths
and your omens.
I declare my love to you Guatemala
when you bury your living with bouganvilleas and the
fluorescent lights of the South.

IV

A country touched by wrath
infinitely torn
by the devourers,
by the merchants
of your fruits
and looms,
a country gagged,
partitioned
in the darkest of darkness
of the night.

V

I approach you
and kiss the branches of your face,
the fertility of your
tongue
that is the word
of the living.

VI

I declare
my love to you Guatemala
I celebrate your birds,
the sound of your ancient wind,
the silent footsteps of
the rocks
and from the south
I see how the fire in your belly lights up
to light our way.

SCHEHERAZADE

Tansparent in an abysmal
sanity,
Scheherazade
approaching the sultan's lips
the sultan's ear
thus allowing each word
to escape like the most
precious rite
of all sounds.
During the nights consumed by terror
words were the vessels of life,
breath was the essence
of being born,
so terribly tender before the fear
they were capable of inventing desire
of removing the perverse ruins of false love.

JUANA INES

Juana
lady of mine
and of all beloved women
distant and hallucinated
magician of verse,
stranger to time,
barefoot among the
convents.
On what night of wrath and jaguars
did you give away your instruments?
Why did you choose
the muteness of the humble?
Who incited you to punish yourself,
to give away the highest jewels of
your knowledge,
the sequins of verse
and keep only the wounds behind the windows
with spellbound shrouds covering the darkness
of your shaved hair?
Why did
death so merry
take away your light?

TO VIRGINIA WOOLF

Virginia with colored stones
or maybe talismans made of words
you approach the river of memory,
to the fangs of wrath
and you sink tranquil and diurnal
and you let the water wrap you
to the last of your rooms,
Virginia so beautiful and small, murky in the waters.

XOCHAQUETZAL, THE GODDESS OF FLOWERS

I

In the times of astonishment
and fugitive flowers,
there you were
Xochaquetzal
all dressed in
flowers
all dressed in sleep
and the blooming orange blossoms
of wars and peace.

II

Tangled in
love,
you covered the earth
with a splendid freshness
of aromas.

III

When you disobeyed
when you loved the illicit prairie,
they covered you in ashes,
they forced you to cry,
to unhook from your mouth
the wilting pines,
the altars of sorrow.

IV

Xochaquetzal
so beautiful and pained
in the prairies of paradise,
trapped within your sleepless
gaze,
you can no longer look at the sky
and illuminate with your
flowering arms
you are a park of ashes
a statue tied among the
ruins
forced to cry,
to hide in darkness and its veils.

V

But even in the days of love,
in the clandestine
celebrations
of the body that does not
want to become a soul,
there you are
my beloved, my sweet
Xochaquetzal
with your stork eyes
with your gardenia
gaze,
anchored in flowers
that spring from your lacerated
body.

SAPPHO

I

Sappho of Lesbos,
Sappho in the covers
of the rain
snobbish and sweet
handing out the most sinister
domes of her calling
the sweetest fringe
of poetry that is love.

II

Sappho, lonely
accompanied by hail,
rock, metals,
the cities that the winds avoid.

III

Sappho, sharp and small
naked among the words,
oversized and hurried.

IV

Sappho delirious
loved, lover
brilliant in the most earthly of summers
faithful servant of the ambiguity
of time, wind, the face on a canvas of poems,
bird necklaces.

THE CITY OF WOMEN

I

In the city
of women
the fairies preside
the councils of peace.
They carry violets and lilacs,
the yellow scepters
of sunflowers
and in their words
they have left behind
the shadows of the
wars,
the precipices of wrath.

II

In the city of women
the children still play astonished.
There are no knives
nor tools to kill;
there are only the hands illuminating the larks,
and the wounded;
only the hands for the memories.

III

In the city
of women,
the men do not hit them.
Nobody tears off their
clothes.
Nobody twists
their wrists.

Nobody drags them by the
hair to the
public fairs.

IV

In the city of women
the borders are only
the meditations of the colorful and
imaginary maps;
there are only thresholds
and balconies of summer,
a council of fairies and apparitions,
of owls painted crimson.

V

In the city of women,
they live among the gestures of love
and they live inventing words and rounded alphabets.
They are all like paradise, like Eden,
like life.

MALINCHE

I

At dawn you descend
among the owls.
There you are, marvelous child,
barefoot among the barefoot.
Ambiguous is you name
like your lineage.
They called you Malinalli,
Marina with the sign of
history,
Malinche, for your enemies and
friends.

II

Who are you marvelous child
in the blue markets?
Among miraculous tiaras,
tea leaves and herbs
which foretell fate,
among the dogs,
and the savage sun of Tabasco,
they sold you, barefoot girl
to a stranger among strangers
like the husbands
who share the sleep
and the insomnia of drowsy
sex.

III

You were shrewd
with words,
you possessed so many voices,
bilingual in the messages of power
and of love.

IV

You accomplished, marvelous sorceress,
a darkened destiny,
always translating,
transfigured for others,
sold by your mother,
seduced among strangers,
accosted and mute among the rocks.

V

So much silence and ease
in your story of inverted symbols.
Ambiguous was your presence,
each time more alive among the
living.
Today I conjure your word,
I celebrate all your names
and I call you women, sliding
alone in the prairies,
barefoot woman
with the calling of the absent.

VI

Transfigured by history,
stranger among your people
your are like all women:
alone
in the prairies.

Sisters

TO SPEAK WITH THE DEAD

to Jorge Tellier

I

To speak with the dead, said Jorge,
one must choose the time of patience,
when the afternoon blends in with the confused sky,
when the birds go back to the thresholds.
Only then
it is convenient to sit down
and wait for them
with their favorite drinks
their favorite magazines.
It is necessary to stay calm and restful,
remain peaceful,
because they are afraid
of returning, of that humid darkness,
they are like children,
learning the first rhythms of
feet and words.

II

It is convenient, said Jorge,
to avoid lights too bright
and to be in the warm penumbra of amber.
When they approach you,
choose the soft texture of certain words
so they can recognize the alphabet of the living
do not get too close to them,
because they are fearful and cold.
Then,
in the fog of fertile time
you will see them approach your warmth
with ancient and golden clothes
like old kings from other worlds
you will see them all lit up
you will see them alive.

COME

I

Come,
move closer as if in a breath
come,
so much time without seeing you
and finally you return from the walls of fear
from the gagged crypts of silence
come,
here I am open
and drunk with stories
awaiting you.

II

Here is my love like a field of green lamps like
a field
of that which is warm.
Come closer
let's make a list of the secret
zones,
of the times you will not leave my generous body.
Your body, like a glass of water that slides down the fingers
and the lips.
You have returned
you have brought me memory.
In your eyes I see a bunch of white lilies,
a bird in love.

III

Come closer,
you no longer are the tortured body.
You have returned to your name,
you have known how to keep in your arms the softness of love,
the craft of loving.
Here I also await you.
I have waited for days, mornings, imaginary nights.
I have gone to bed with the memory of your bones,
I feel them like maps without a memory.
I have loved your empty clothes filled with holes.

IV

Come,
you have returned from the hell
of hells
nobody could take
your life.

THE WIDOWS OF IOWA

I

The widows of Iowa
with their hats
of gold and their
blue eyes travel behind the fields,
beyond the moss,
they are ephemeral like the seasons of silence,
golden like those slow places
where silence grows hallucinating
before the vastness of the light among the shadows.

II

There they are
collecting wheat
overflowing with memories
sitting in the thresholds
petting the nearby animals
murmuring about their widowhood
about the ephemeral travels through the distances:
Iowa, Minnesota, Indiana.

III

The map of America is so desolate,
immense and mean,
the women are the threads that weave
a loneliness even more daring.

IV

I see them
and I like to listen to them
as they collect postcards,
tickets from dead trains
or they exchange fake recipes
of the places where they
could have been
free
without veiling their words.
I like to listen to them,
they review photo albums
of all detained
seasons
and they smile.

V

Among the prairies,
they brush their hair
which is a vanishing thread.
The widows of Iowa
swinging with the restless wind of the South;
the widows of Iowa
mingling with the corn fields,
with the silence,
with the pain of ambiguous time.

THE WIDOWS OF THE DESERT

I

Like fugitives
with arched shapes,
the widows
approach the desert.
At that silent crossroads,
in that immense and open thickness
they also grow
like green plants behind the hallucinations,
like grass in the languid prairies.

II

From the blooming desert
like a crown of dead violets,
they also call the dead,
they know how to approach their footprints,
they touch them as if they were warm and moving sands.

III

In the deserts, where they are
because they can be heard there,
because their footprints there are
like infinite avatars ,
they are easily confused
with the long walks of the dead,
with the flowers that during the night
bloom
to ward the dead.
The night of
the desert
warms them.

THE WOMEN OF BOSNIA

I

Fragile, punished
the wanderers
arrived to the borders.
They carried their children
tied to their hearts;
they carried their thimbles
with the sings of blood.

II

I saw them approach the
cities,
they were hungry,
they were cold;
they were good women
like those who
facilitated food in the days
of scarcity.

III

They were neither strangers nor foreigners,
since, as you can see, from their wombs were born
those children.
They had given birth like you, like me.
How strange not to see them,
even stranger not to hear them
howling
for a little water
to place on the lips
of the children.

IV

You also know
what it is like to travel with
the children,
the desperation
of the journeys,
but one always dreams of the arrivals,
but, what do they dream of?
The refugees of this war, of all wars.

V

They have been told to return to their cities,
but there are simply no cities left after the war,
it is as simple as death,
as luminous as life
this truth of the refugees without shelter.

VI

Do you know that they cannot return
there is no home, or neighbor
there are no gardens or lemon trees?
They are not a bunch of faces
those who call at your door,
they are neighbors, housewives, actresses,
poets, merchants of eggs and fish.

VII

They could
be your friends,
or does poverty scare you?
does dark skin bother you?

They could be the teachers
of your children;
they could be your sisters.

VIII

Go,
let them in,
give them the charity of water,
offer them a tablecloth of poppies
rescue them from the darkness.
Be good for a moment,
not only in the house of God,
but here, in your home.
They have come to see you,
open your door to them and you will see
without fear
do not fear if they seem dead,
give them the water of charity, pray for the living
and you will see.

THE WOMEN OF WAR

I

The women of war
with the fallen angels
carry reddish wings,
make tattoos on the arched
backs.
The women of war
with baskets of poppies
and dead heads,
dance among the rubbish
of the dead.

II

The women of war
with their baskets of poppies
and their aprons stained by the
blood of their dead.
The women of war
buy golden shoes.
They have already learned
to converse with
death.

THE WOMEN OF SARAJEVO

I

In Sarajevo
the snow weaves fragile paths,
approaching the roads,
leaving its bloody steps,
the transparency of its hollow gaze.
It snows in Sarajevo,
the dead do not know where to seek shelter.
It snows in Sarajevo and the winter is like a heart
among the black shadows.
Very far away...very close by
the footsteps of the living
making alliances with the
dead.
A finger from the corpse
drawing hearts.

II

In Sarajevo
this winter
the women caress the
harps of the night,
the eyelids of the night.
They dream with fruits from the South,
arpeggios,
they feed themselves with that very deep sound
from the piano
in the midst of the night that ruminates,
that moves
to scare the dead.

III

This winter it will snow copiously in Sarajevo.
Suspiciously it will snow in Sarajevo.
The living will know how and why they make love,
somebody will write poetry on the frost
because they will not be able to speak,
because no one will see them in their transparency,
because snow is a sacred silence.

IV

In Sarajevo
the children also die
and they do not die in automobile accidents.
It snows copiously
and the dead do not know where to seek shelter.
The women caress
the harps
of the night.

THE WOMEN OF THE RIVER

I

The women of the river,
looking through the enchantments
of the river's edge;
the women of the river,
among all the land's rivers:
fragile, arched
like all the seconds,
like the roundness of the river itself.
There go the women of the rolling river.
They go to the river to cry
and their skirts are made of water and the thick humidity of algae.

II

That's how the women of the river are.
They approach the edges of life,
shredding death.
The women of the river carry
the skirts of love in their insides,
The resounding women of the river,
daily and mute.
The women of the river with
faces like dragonflies;
the women of the river defying
the fear of the
whirlwinds
and all the islands
and all the sands of the water.

THE WOMEN OF LOVE

Drowned in sorrows
and little shipwrecks
the women
in love,
with their cold breasts,
approach the sea
torn,
sleepless.
They disappear behind
the coasts
the heavy fogs.

SHE

She covered her hair with ashes
my sister Eva or Sofia,
her eyes filled with birds that returned to her sleepy hands,
she was filled with blue water and began to speak about miracles,
she used the rites of the Christian sisters,
kneeling she inserted some dirt into her mouth
where only memory surrounded her
where all the rooms closed down like something evil and austere.

They had arrived to Auschwitz
and in the fields plowed
by all the empty rumors
she also repeated
the names of other
sisters,
ancestors and lineages.

She had arrived to Auschwitz.
In the distance a branch bloomed
among the rubble,
and it approached the silent sound
of the wind that had
the smell of death.

In the distance, the dead sisters arrived,
they made reverences to the dead,
they sat down to snack on the now holy ground.

Somebody cleaned the ashes from her mouth.
They did no ask her for words,
they did not ask her to step forth to tell them
the names
nor to ask them about the roofs made of ashes.

THE SISTERS

I

There were neither trees
nor oblivion,
the underbrush eroded the air
there were no birds
only empty time
and forests that had sunk in the blue amber
of death.

II

When they arrived,
there was nothing but
the Epiphany of memory,
clear memories, the sacred
memories
of the dead
who seemed to be hollow and uninhabited, strewn about the poppy
fields.

III

When they arrived,
the fog seemed to be a greedy and evil witch
the angel of death awaited,
and shrouded them in moans.

IV

They had arrived to the field
of intrepid death,
my sisters
had crossed nonexistent
frontiers,
they had made up successful journeys,
to be there
and, what was that "there,"
that disinterred city of the
dead?
together with the surprised
living
before what could be seen in the soil, as well as out in
the open, in the shadows and the wakes.

THE HAND

I

Approach
without a care,
approach
and give me the
hand.
You will see that although
it is smaller
and covered by the clefts
of many imaginary
journeys,
it looks like yours.

II

It intertwines with
the greatness of yours.
Intertwined, they
cannot be distinguished,
they are like sisters of the same tribe
of century-old ancestors
and some times, they are confused
as if they were one river or one nation
lit up with lighthouses.

III

Do not be afraid,
there is nothing more
earth-shattering
than the shuddering
of tenderness,
that trembling of love.
Give me your hand

and without any hurry,
as if you were lighting
all the lamps,
as if darkness
were a lost lady.

IV

I like your hand on
mine, so still,
like a mouth on another mouth,
or a song in
another language.
I like to feel the beating of
its texture on mine
blood like and artery where all delusion feeds into.
I like to feel it and to have you squeeze it
because we are alive.

V

This is neither the time
for wars
nor false alliances.
This is not the time
for a hand over the other,
for a ring
mingling with
another.

VI

I like to feel the beating
of your hand
when you greet me
or when you closes the eyelids of
the dead,

the lost passengers.
I like your hand
when you make up foods
or write a song.

VII

They are so similar:
twenty fingers,
left and right,
twenty nails
that grow after
death.

VIII

Look at the hands
they are like
small mounts.
I fill mine
with bands
and rings,
of your gifts.

IX

I like you to
give me your hand.
It is alive like
a secret ceremony,
clear like amber,
capable of holding my body
or the fragility of a finger,
capable of inventing a word
and holding a child's nape.

X

Give me your hand,
dance with me.
'Give me your hand
and find me.
Give me your hand
to receive
the branch, the
wind,
the secret,
all the signals
of love.
Come,
approach,
do not fear.
Your hand
fits within mine
it is a fleeting night
it is your mouth on mine.

THE WEAVER

The weaver
wakes up,
with her colorful hive.
She herself seems to be
the color of love.
She is careful about threading her needle,
not forgetting her thimble,
the weaver looked
for dreams and tapestries.
She finds herself
in the amber-colored blankets,
in the agate-colored yarns.
I like to see her creating schemes,
secret passages, family alliances,
imagining that her fingers are trees of naked women
the color
of love.

THE CITIES OF WOMEN

PRAYER

I

A woman among the sleepiest
solitudes
makes a phone call
and is answered
with obscenities.
Another one goes to
the brother
and assures him that she has
no money
for the abortion,
let her bleed to death
he says.

II

A woman
buys milk and rice
they make fun of her,
of her pronounced belly,
of her varicose leg,
of her generous homeliness.

III

A woman gives birth in a sinister
county hospital
they insult her
because she loved her unhinged sex
they leave her
alone and she moans at the emptiness,
torn in the flatlands.

IV

A woman goes to
a hotel
she needs the gratuitous caress,
a caress
and he opens her legs
and rips
her heart.

V

A woman commits suicide
on the sidewalks
and the passers-by
are very irate
with her pious
gesture.

VI

A woman
howls, she goes
on a hunger strike
they throw rocks at her,
they tell her she is a witch
and they spit at her.

VII

A woman
awaits
behind the rivers,
she awaits the time of the winds
she likes to create the
seasons
of summer.

VIII

A woman is
afraid
and her job

is a silence
a begging
among the vanities.

IX

A woman
asks that they look at her in the eye
and she can only see the mirrors behind the shadows,
an echo among
the pack of hounds.

X

A woman
builds
a city,
a blooming desert.

WOMEN

I

I never favored
statistics
nor measuring tapes.
I preferred the disorganized rhythm
of lethargic time,
the drowsiness of joyous heat.
However,
it is necessary to clarify,
repeat,
invoke,
even to the point of painful and indifferent weariness,
that every fifteen seconds
they rape a woman,
they quarter her,
they pierce her gaze,
they shred her hair,
they steal her bleeding heart
and in their meticulous
homes,
with elaborate gardens
without pretense,
when darkness shows up like a thorny hand,
one of every five
women
is dragged
to the sweaty floor,
slapped,
disfigured,
in a forest tinged with civilized delirium.

II

Ninety percent
of refugees are women.
Haven't you seen them on TV
while you have cereal or fried eggs for breakfast?
or while you study the books of poverty
in those luxurious hotels of the third world?

III

One percent
of the exiguous wealth
of the planet
is property
of us women,
and the rest:
he plants,
the rock formations,
the water,
belong to the "lords" of war,
to the patriarchs with stained uniforms,
the ones who after the sumptuous dinners
descend to the cellars
because they
enjoy
watching how
they torture
the nun from El Salvador,
or the Muslim woman
from Bosnia
or the white woman
from Ohio.

IV

Statistics
do not lie,
nor do they
present
false evidence,.
They are the
loyal witnesses
without means,
without ears,
without eyes.
They are the luxury of excess.

AN EGYPTIAN GIRL

An Egyptian girl
with headbands and white lilies
came
to celebrate
Passover.
She dipped her tiny fingers
in the sad herbs, savage and salty.
She shuddered
before the bone
on the Seder dish.
She reclined
and knew that this night
was unlike all other nights
because on that table
confused among the rites,
we had crossed over the omens of peace.

An Egyptian girl
came
to my dinner, to my house.
She dipped her fingers in the bitter herbs
and told me,
as if in a song
or a prayer,
that she had also
left Egypt.

THE WOMEN WHO WAIT

The women
in the thresholds of darkness,
slow and sure, making footsteps
in the darkness.
The women bent over near the river,
washing with love the sleepy rocks,
searching in the tides
for the names
of the dead.
The women near the rivers;
the women near
the seas;
the women and life
awaiting.

THE SECRETARY

The secretary
with her tedious attires
keying,
the same memo that
she duplicates in her tanned hands.
She is one exhausted
mistress of the system:
obedient, disciplined,
methodical in her responses
but when five o'clock comes
she open the heart
of her perfectly buttoned blouse,
she opens the sheets of fire
that label her no longer clean heart.
The secretary leaves her captivity,
she goes to the distant parking lot
where the sweet alcohol awaits her
and she wanders towards the lucky bars
where nobody names her, where nobody my recognize her
to create another life, away from the land of ink and erasure.

ANGELS
to Elena Gascón Vera

I

Women do look alike,
they are round and winged,
with burning cheeks.

II

They are messengers of salt and love,
guardians of the rooms
of the sky,
protectors of the dead,
friends of the children and the
sick.
They arrive to the most remote places
of the savage heart,
like the clarity of the arpeggios.
They are not friends of death in its perpetual greed.

THE COLLECTOR

More than words,
she collected prophecies,
their lascivious cadences,
their feathers, drifting
in the ambiguity of words.

More than words
I love their textures,
shiny,
disorganized,
like hearts sprouting
from the roundness of moss,
in the snowy desert
of silence.

SEAMSTRESS DURING THE DAY

I

I wake up
early.
I feed
my children,
I cover myself completely
with darkened
clothes
and attires.

II

Nothing reveals
my fragrance
nor the gardenias in my hair.
I work,
I organize,
I fast.

III

I am meticulous in the cleaning of
the back rooms.
I smooth out the sheets,
I iron them eternally
to erase the face of the pubis that sunk in them.

IV

I wax the leaves of autumn,
I lull to sleep the smells of all eves,
I kill birds and chickens,

I feed my children again,
I work on my sewing.
I sew my dolls,
I darn my lips.
I do not stop sewing.
I sew containers to
hold my
tongue,
to save the hairs of
my soul,
to save the
mouths of love,
to save my ears.

V

Dusk falls,
I cover myself with my nightgown of dross,
filled with dead skins.
My husband kisses me
and I kiss him
asleep.
He does not recognize me.

VI

Like one of Dali's molten clocks
I open my legs
and sigh.
He falls asleep
I know I fulfilled my duty.
I breastfeed my youngest daughter,
it is twelve midnight,
the time of fairies and the dead.

VII

I write poems.
The words are faces,
they are fireflies
in love
with threads of
shimmering water.

VIII

Happiness
is in knowing
how to apply verses
with my pubis.
I write and I am
exhausted from
the beauty
of saying.
I say reddish things, mauve ones, violet ones.
With frenzy I make love
with the poems.
I yell that I love poetry and the exhausted stretch between syllables,
I am happy.
It is dawn and verse has nested in me, it seems to be a drunken
swallow.

IX

It dawns.
I return to the rooms of the century-old sacred families.
I wake up early,
I poison my children,
I pray.

THE MAIDS

I

The maids,
yesterday's relics,
living in the back rooms:
in a fearsome darkness,
eating leftovers,
other's children
and borrowed ones,
children hidden in the skylight
of bad love.

II

The aids,
the *cholas,*
the little Indians,
in borrowed palaces,
cleaning up feces,
making curtsies,
serving fresh coffee twenty-four hours a day,
and martinis twenty-four hours a day.
Obeying the orders of the naked precocious
youth that, tempted,
chooses arrogance instead of desire
and simply penetrates her body
following the customs
of lineage,
filled with the haughtiness
of his lineage,
the haughtiness
of the penis,
the games of his lineage.

Breathing heavily, the maid,
the Indian, the country whore,
sleepy,
breeds the child
of others,
eats the food
of others,
drinks the air of
others
and thus lives
in fear, dead
among the ashes,
with the cross
of wheat
with the new
life
like a
grave.

THE LADIES OF THE NIGHT

The ladies of the night
disinhabit their bodies
tied in their silence
that cannot be heard,
nailed to the face of love
in the nights
when they are
not named.

LLORONA[1]

I

As if lost,
as if howling
sleepwalking through the parties,
as if torn
the *llorona* threw them
into the river.
The *llorona* tied them up
to scare them away
from life.
The *llorona*
loved them
and in the insanity
without love
she rocked them in the river
of the dead angels.
This *llorona* of Carolina,
this *llorona* is a drowned lost soul
in her will she is enchanted,
inhabited by teetering shadows.

II

The *llorona*
is tied up,
they ask for the electric
chair for
the *llorona*.
They want this blond *llorona*
in the bonfire.

[2] *"Llorona" literally means "crying woman." It is the name of a legend in which a woman drowned her own children in a river and then went insane. Supposedly, she shows up every night by the river and cries out for her children.*

The people, the nation,
the men of the earth,
beg for justice
but, who has had justice
for the blindfolded women,
those who steal food,
rice, drops of milk,
the women of Bosnia and Dachau?
Who has pity for
the female crew members
of raped nights?
What for do they dream, barefoot, in the shelters,
the psychiatric wards?
The *llorona* threw her children
to the river.
The *llorona* feels.
The *llorona*
is sorry.
The *llorona*
does not go to the river
to search for
her children.
The *llorona* no longer cries
and we
throw
stones at her,
we beg
for the souls of the disappeared,
but the truth is gentlemen:
when the *llorona*
walked by
begging for the nourishment
of love,
for a kind word,
nobody
opened their doors
to the *llorona*.
Nobody washed
her feet
or her hands,

or kissed the
children,
lost in a
mute land.
The *llorona*
does not cry
does not search
she threw them
in the river
long ago.
The *llorona*
does not cry,
you cry for her.

KNIVES

I

In the humidity of the night,
in the hoarse and well-defined night,
a woman approaches her silences.
Her clothes are imbued with the rhythm of sorrow
and she is also the silence of bony knives.

II

In the humidity of dark rooms
in the darkest and most well-hidden recesses of time,
a woman forgets love,
the lost objects of love,
the imaginary caresses
in the absence of marked and distant skin.
In the moist night
a woman calls herself and moans.

THE GLOBE
TO JOY

I

She gave me
the world in a globe,
it fit within the
fleeting quality
of my hands,
it was round
nocturnal and diurnal
full of holes and eternal,
blue like the wild winds and seas,
it had rivers in love with the thickness,
green and intrepid mountains,
it had eagles and fish in love,
a jaguar and a heliotrope.
I watched it in awe
it looked like a small star
yearning for shelter,
carefully I approached the heart of its thickness
so round it was
I wanted to show it the duties of love,
I wanted to fill it with warmth.

II

I did not recognize the countries,
the globe did not belong to anyone other than
my sleepy
hands
which held it
only to gaze at it
and love it.

III

This globe seemed to be
spectacularly beautiful
finely perfect,
so naked and full
of light,
so nocturnal with its lizards, the iguanas of the night
the scent of darkness and a desire like mauve dragonflies.

IV

My friend Joy
has given me
the globe
without the school's geography
with which we dilute forms,
with the touch
of dissipated wars
which are the inventions of shadowy nightmares.

V

The globe
fit within my hands
the dreams filtered through the rain,
how I like the Earth,
it is the true paradise
subject to the scent, the
breath, the perfection of love.
I shelter myself in the green
of memory's dreams.
I like the Earth
its ambiguous texture,
its errors
its similarities to the moon,
the love struck Mediterranean.
I like the violet desert, its echoes.

This gift,
tiny and moving,
it fits within my hands
I lull it to sleep near my heart
and its magical beating.
I love the Earth
and I belong to it.
I sink my hands
in the warm and hazy
core.

MEN

I

Men say
that one night
of love
justifies making war.

II

Men say
that the yellow frontiers
of the maps
must be defended until the
death itself of geography.

III

Men say
that envy and lust
are necessary.

IV

Men say that the death
of our children is inevitable
during war.

V

Women say
that men should give birth
thus nothing would justify those wars
in the name of a night of love.

SEX

I

The first wet kiss,
brief, small,
like a firefly scared
by the passing of sorrows
and days.

II

I thought about the body intertwined with another,
one half woven into the other
and it would last more than an hour
maybe all night long,
I was wrong.
Love was fast and restless
like an advertisement.
I was disappointed in the word orgasm
which implied too much agony and
too many *rs* and *ms*
I have yet to figure out what it really is
could it be a German dish?

III

In my old age
sex seems to be
uncomplicated
and lacking in ambiguity
it has no secrets
or secretions,
it happens in a predictable manner
in predictable places.

IV

I would like to love at the bottom of the sea
with a cricket orchestra,
on a mattress of golden leaves,
I would like to love in an imaginary city
naked, I would build monuments without history
only to be delirious and
search for another soul like
mine, disillusioned
by the tyrannies of desire.
How I would like
for you
to simply touch my heart.

SEX II

I

Sex
like the cave of chance
perfumed in the muteness
of love
that blossoms like the
naive beating
of butterflies.

II

Sex, astonished
and intrepid
making the greatest pleasure
before habit,
before the breath of that other
alien and familiar,
brother and enemy,
surprised and everyday.
Sex like a
country;
the room of discoveries.

I CRY

I used to cry less
two or three times a year
when I would lose the list
for the potatoes and tomatoes
when I felt the restless omen
of the dead.
Now I cry more
and I am happy.
I cry with emotion when I wake up
and when I smile as our sweet air
climbs the restless sheets.
I cry when my daughter Sonia smiles
with her beacon eyes
with her hands made of water and rivers.
I cry when they defy me,
I cry when they accuse me,
I cry when I repeat the word mauve,
I cry when I think of a very tall man who does not write me love
letters,
I cry when I get a cold
and when I get my period,
when they call me on the phone,
I cry when someone tells me they love me
and that I have been useful
since I cry incessantly
I have regained
happiness.

MY MOTHER

My mother is
 a ghost accompanying me
in my journeys.
My mother
has islands in her eyes
and curly copper-colored hair.
She walks as if
she were made of water,
as if she had just woken up
from dreams.
I listen to her
while she caresses my hand
while she covers me with times and words.
In her it seems that I arrive to all savage ports.
My mother has islands in her eyes and hands of a garden.
Beside her I write and I am.

MOTHERS

Irene Santibáñez
René Eppelbaum
Lía Dusovsky
wanderers
walking among the air and the sky,
evasive,
wandering, immobile
where are you going
with your amber faces,
with your hands like rain
with the islands of peace
in your hair?
Where do you go on tiptoe
immobile wanderers,
lost elves, burnt fairies?
Who do you call with faint and delirious voices?
How tired you look with your faces like cracked nations.
You have been walking for almost twenty years.
Who are you looking for
in the darkness?
Who do you call with the mumbling
language
of love?
Sailors on the islands of peace,
mourning women with white handkerchiefs,
so much patience among the shadows,
so many mournings throughout the years,
but here they are, Irene, Angelina,
bent over like the most remote circle,
with the closest circle,
searchers of children and men,
seers,
ladies of transparency,
fragile, holding up half of the sky,
looking toward the most ephemeral distances
toward the place where the sun always sets
calling them with the names of the living.

ALL WOMEN ARE FAT

All women
are fat,
even the most anorexic ones,
even the tiniest ones.
All women
are fat,
they savor
life in installments,
the last instant of a mouthful,
they eat in spurts,
having a sweet tooth and being disorganized,
in a hurry.
All women
are fat,
but they no longer suffer
for food,
only for the scarcity
of them;
only for the children of wars,
for the diabetic nuns.

WOMEN CHOOSE MEN

Women choose
men.
They are the ones
who authorize
up to what point the kiss,
tongue and sex can go.
Women choose
men.
Although astutely
they act
to be chosen.

Women choose
men,
maddened by solitude
they seek them
through the never-sleeping cities
and they request the only possible offer:
the naked body
dazzling, always ready
for the chances of love.

40

At the
age of
forty,
I advise
irreverence,
the wonderful clumsiness
of joyful
imprudence.
I advise
walking barefoot
through the apple trees
during moonlit
nights.

II

Eating ice-cream with whipped cream,
instead of
fluorescent lettuce,
instead of dead lettuce.

At forty
I advise
long walks
on hidden paths,
creating well-lit
caves,
telling fairy tales
with new endings,
looking for animals
to wander,
to be lamps,
within the hidden foliage
of the storks.

At the age of
forty I advise:
lust,
the silence of the noble,
a barn owl,
an eagle owl,
the marvelous lamp of unmoving time.

WHEN I GROW UP

I

When I grow up
I won't be a married
and luxurious lady
in an empty palace.
I will not review electric
bills
nor open my legs
at midnight to the rhythm
of the clock every Thursday.
I will not go to the bathroom and close the door.
I will not weep before my daunting nakedness.

II

When I grow up
I will not marry
a skinny man
who snores,
and who spends
Sundays immersed
in beers
and football games,
who does not speak
and only moans in his idleness.

III

When I grow up
I will walk naked in the parks,
I will chase squirrels
and madly love
a man who does not

have great wealth,
who has his caring pouch
and who does not have much hair either
but I will love him.

IV

When I grow up
I will make a living
as a poet
or as an apprentice
to dreams,
I will undress
always
to make love,
to breath the lavender breeze,
I will dream of
what could not be,
I will be
a very crazy old lady.
very much in love
with the untamed
core
of love.
I will
never be
a grown
woman,
I will be
a small,
wise,
old lady,
arranging bones,
in love.

THE WIFE

I

The wife practices professions:
the perfect maid,
with the instant and perfect husband
and the squeezed oranges
like miraculous amber drops.

II

Nothing satisfies the mandate
of the master,
then she undresses
and howls.
He laughs at her exuberance,
her body is much too familiar
and remote.
In that belly her now grown children nested.
He has no interest in inseminating her again,
she is flaccid, the golden wife is now
a woman without music
hollow in the distance.

III

She practices professions:
she cuts off the top of an onion
as if it were a bloodless queen,
as if it were a tablecloth of stars.
She sprinkles oregano,
she weaves the tablecloth.

IV

He looks at her full of perfidy
as if she were a stranger
familiar and migratory.

V

He recognizes her face, broken
by all the absences,
he eats and meditates,
retreats to sleep, irate.
She practices
professions:
the lover
that caresses
and he is only a remote
yawn, undressed and sour
dreaming with the body
of the past
with her and none of them.
She dreams of professions
she does not find
the vocation
of being
like they
have made her.
She is uncomfortable
in her clothes,
the mask,
the life,
like a broken
thimble.

THERE ARE WOMEN LIKE THE ANGELS

I

There are women
like the
angels:
transparent,
full of kindness.
There are women
like the angels:
obedient and disobedient,
fed on piety
and celery
water.

II

They are the angels
of eternal life
those willing to die,
to succumb to the laziness
and the idleness
of the human race.

III

Generally they live
alone,
in houses near the abyss
of the sky.

IV

There are women
who are very thin
like the good
angels
and very deaf,
also like the good angels,
companions of the errant night,
Samaritans of love.

V

There are women
like the reddish
angels:
they are plump,
they are robust,
they do not succumb
even to the angel
of demureness,
they are incautious,
unaware,
they like to dress up
in sequins,
with blue rabbit's
tails.

VI

There are women
that are like the angels
of night and day:
they dance in red slippers
although they always seem to fly barefoot,
like the truly pious.

They laugh openly,
they show their imperfections,
they achieve eternal life,
they die in a bed filled with men,
dragonflies and butterflies.

VII

There are women like the angels:
they wear red capes and know how to make love.

HAPPINESS

HAPPINESS

Happiness:
a naked body
in a circle of fog.

Happiness:
a pride of leopards sleeping the sleep of the river.

Give me a piece of happiness
which is your heart:
its pulse like
bubbles and crystal.

Yes, I want it all
and in abundance
more than anything your gaze
fertile and infinite
like the drops of the ocean
that fit within my breath.

Happiness:
a mother with her daughter
reunited in the threshold of sleep
while they hug
losing themselves in the thickness
of the skin.

Happiness:
a healed toothache,
a bottle of wine, loud and crazy.
a party of
seas and marbles
or a stormy sunset
with a green sky.

Happiness:
preparing a garden

with naughtiness,
with the secret touch
of the fair man's earth.

Happiness:
when Dubrovnik slept a night in peace
and I found myself thankful
in its clear scent.

Happiness:
when you sleep
with me all night
and you are
some times
a barefoot river,
a face down archipelago.
Your body lights up completely
like golden eyelids
and in dreams I am, we are,
we dream that all are sheltered this
and every night.

My happiness:
when I find
a word that
I love: lark, traveling bags, alliances;
when I travel the invisible cities.

Your happiness:
when you are wise, welcoming,
when you laugh in thirst.

Happiness:
when the guitar
resurrects
the dead,
calls the dead guests
that clap
among the rocks
because they are air, memory and time.

Happiness:
when you tell me
that you will touch my heart,
that you will look for the balconies of my childhood,
that you will find the princesses' stone,
Doña Helena's inn
Neruda's house,
my water keys.

Happiness:
when writing
I flow and overflow,
when the words are sovereign
and precise,
humble and sophisticated,
beacons that light up
the alphabet
of my happiness;
when the poetry saves me
from lying tongues,
that is my happiness, round
like women.

Sublime
happiness:
when you call me
and wait for me
in the land of ambiguous corners,
in the nation of sounds;
when the forests are filled with witches and angels
because there are no frontiers other
than the clearings in the forests
because all is like a Van Gogh field.

Happiness:
when you turn
everything
into a banquet of new life.

NEW LIFE

to Enrique Lihm and Sonia Helena

I

Sonia Helena
nothing is lost
by living.
Choose
the imperfection
of chance,
the surrounding rhythms
of digressions
and prophecies.
Try and practice
vulnerability.
Be ambiguous
with destiny.
Be generous with
the tyrant,
austere in love.
Teach them to
stretch out a hand
and hang on to the illusion
of the deep,
that is happiness
without a hurry.
Learn to listen to the dead,
and their steps like the march of the tango.

II

Be warm
with those who cry,
with the exiled,
the tortured,
those who migrate
from all cities

and also
let them know
that they carry the landscape of
the nation in their eyes.

III

Sonia Helena,
nothing is lost in
living.
As Enrique used to say,
try,
live life as if it
were always a return
the birthplace of flat waves.
Do not hurry
because we have all the time in the world.

IV

At the times
of insomnia,
when you sail and you are
a disturbed shadow,
choose poetry
because it, as well as
prayer, will know how
to be your guardian angel
and verse will be for you
a feather
on the lip
of your God.

V

More than to survive,
choose to live life like the air,
with all its sinister risks.
Make offerings to the birds of the earth,
to the greenness,
to the trunk of the abyss.
Foster rites, the ceremonies of love.
Abandon all empty rites.
Hide all the amulets, the envy and possible pettiness.

VI

Do not be too
cautious,
or too severe with yourself,
or wish for great
achievements,
or palaces of wind.
Do not forget that
happiness
is only
a hand,
a sigh,
to give
a violet.

VII

Nothing is lost
in living
Sonia Helena,
with trying.
Sonia Helena,
daughter, friend,
choose life.

THE GENERALS

I

When they asked me
why I did not write about
the generals,
I restlessly delayed
my answer.
Cautiously I told them
that their names were
so long they did not rhyme
with the splendor
of words,
that their capes
were too somber.

II

When they insisted
as to why there wasn't a single
dictator in my verses,
I responded
that they did not like poetry much,
that they split before those ephemeral and strangely rolling words
that I could not mention them in my poems.
Then they insisted,
with the prudence of the mediocre.
Then I told them
that generals do not know
how to dance.

POETRY

I

Poetry,
like the alchemy
of the palate:
savage, golden and wild,
leaves the hand
full of sayings,
leaves the tongue,
speaks and moans.
Poetry, like the knife
that slices the subtle blush
of the tomato,
the hallucinating moss,
the divine neatness of the elegant asparagus.

II

Surprised, poetry alights in the familiar room,
she is the welcome guest
at any time
at the tables of purified clay and porcelain,
true to foods, to beverages,
it springs like the knife,
from my
hand, like
the tongue
that is delirious
in the heart
of the word.

WOMEN'S WORD

How I love the alphabets.
I learn to disappear in them.
I conjugate time backwards.
I approach the veil of memories,
words.
How they make me kneel to the breath of life
and within them I name thee
and within them I undress completely,
anxious,
to tell you
that it is a smoking syllable
in the heart of my tongue.

THE WORD

Alphabets
explode within me
the sacred writings
grass, mud, the time of winds,
of sayings
and I tell you
that I love words
when I approach them in desperation
blooming with sounds to call you.

WOMEN'S TASKS

I

Poetry chose me
it recognized my
lack of ability
for the management
of real estate
and other grave and scary
causes.

II

Poetry
knew about my incoherence,
my forgetful
passions for disloyal men.
Poetry understood
my inability for technological
tasks
but it new I liked the
laptop computer
and electronic kisses.
It knew I liked
to make poetry as well as to travel,
to speak with my dead and living
and to carry the
words
on my lap,
write them on
backs,
feel the heartbeat
of the earth,
imagine salamanders
making love.

III

Of all tasks
I write verses.
While forgetful
I watch over my children
I think about the boiled rice.
Poetry fits in with maternity:
it is so soft and tenebrous,
it likes the time of silences and solstices
when all sleep
and the words sharpen themselves like outrageous knives
in the sinister
and presumably beautiful
night.

IV

Poetry is
my portable
task,
like a computer,
it is light in blood
it arrives at the most unexpected moments,
it is not unwelcome
nor evil,
but rather it foretells
like Cassandra,
weaves and unweaves like Penelope,
it could be crazily in love like Beatrice
and more than anything it is a celestial
enchantress of all thimbles and syllables,
of all the virgins never mended.

Poetry is my
task.

CELEBRANT OF LOVES

Of all
possible
tasks,
of all erroneous and precise
vocations
I will tell you
that I would stay with
the tasks of love:
uncontrolled, ambiguous,
delirious,
love in a nocturnal plaza.

Of all possible
tasks
I will stay with love:
rounded, dancing, at the edge of the abyss,
lacking sense and breathing hard;
fugitive, runaway love
clandestine;
love like destiny,
like poetry imbedded in the swollen
cleft of the heart,
like an imperial topaz.

ABSENCE

I

Absence
they called her.
Her body was
a pure clay,
molded by
the loneliness
of the dawns.

II

Absence
they called her
and she was the harvester
of hidden voices,
a translucent woman
among the landscapes,
falling on the grass,
the sky,
the hidden firmament that
undressed her in the fog.

WRITER

She loves the
vanishing cities,
that which is ashen and
ambiguous memory.
She loves absences,
the walk of that
which is seemingly lost.
She loves passion,
that which is not
but is the closest
thing to words,
to the lost tongue.
She loves the signs before the gestures.
She perfumes herself
before saying anything.
On tiptoe
she enters the rooms of findings
and she counts in
silence
as if each word
were secret
lace.

EPITAPH
allegro

For my epitaph
don't talk about the elongated beauty
of my words.
I beg with the entreaty of the dead:
do not say
"she was an illustrious poet."
I only ask that you tell
that I liked to be a tourist,
to buy toys and doves,
fill my room with damned
souvenirs,
that I liked interior design,
wearing the color red,
falling in love with
the ungrateful
and writing poetry at midnight
on the strong back of my teenage,
eighty year-old,
middle-aged boyfriends,
lame and confused.
Yes, my boyfriends,
that had little to do
with poetry
or the path
of the intellect.
They were technocrats
bankers
and poor tourists,
of course,
passers-by in love,
light and trembling.
I, through them,
knew about poetry and dark loves.
joy in life.
Death is but a
friendly neighbor.